ORIGAMI
Step by Step

Robert Harbin

DOVER PUBLICATIONS, INC.
Mineola, New York

My grateful thanks to all those folders who have contributed models for this book, and especially Patricia Crawford of the United States of America, who has allowed me to illustrate so many of her remarkable creations.

Published in Canada by General Publishing Company, Ltd., 30 Lesmill Road, Don Mills, Toronto, Ontario.
Published in the United Kingdom by Constable and Company, Ltd., 3 The Lanchesters, 162–164 Fulham Palace Road, London W6 9ER.

Bibliographical Note

This Dover edition, first published in 1998, is an unabridged, slightly amended republication of the text and diagrams from *Origami: A Step-by-Step Guide,* first published in Great Britain in 1974 by The Hamlyn Publishing Group Ltd. An updated bibliography and a revised index have been added.

Library of Congress Cataloging-in-Publication Data

Harbin, Robert, 1909–
    Origami step by step / Robert Harbin.
        p.   cm.
    Rev. ed. with updated bibliography of: Origami. 1974.
    Includes bibliographical references and index.
    ISBN 0-486-40136-7 (pbk.)
    1. Origami.   I. Harbin, Robert, 1909–   Origami.   II. Title.
TT870.H318   1998
736'.982—dc21   98-10715
                                                                                        CIP

Manufactured in the United States of America
Dover Publications, Inc., 31 East 2nd Street, Mineola, N.Y. 11501

Contents

Introduction 4

Before You Begin 5

Symbols 7

Flower 8

Japanese Box 11

Water-Bomb Base 12

Church 13

Fancy Box 13

Salt Cellar 14

Lover's Knot 14

Anvil 15

Super-Box 15

Guillemot 16

Tetrahedron 18

Decoration 20

Yacht 21

Speedboat 22

Dart 23

Lakotoi 24

"No Walk Today" 25

Two Nuns 26

Film Star 27

Octahedron 28

Bellows 29

Stalking Cat 30

Birdbath 32

Squirrel on a Log 35

Birds in a Nest 39

Mermaid 42

Christ on the Mount of Olives 45

Swan 47

Unicorn 49

Kangaroo 52

Scorpion 55

Full-rigged Ship 58

Stand for Ship 60

Bibliography and Organizations 61

Index 63

Introduction

Origami is a Japanese word which means paper-folding. For many hundreds of years the Japanese have cultivated this art form.

During the past four decades origami has become a sophisticated Western pastime, and countless new models have been created in the United States, Great Britain, Europe, and the Latin American countries.

All you need is a piece of foldable paper and an idea in mind, and sooner or later something delightful will evolve.

Origami Step by Step will lead you gently into this old and very exciting world. If you manage to make every model described in this book you will indeed be a folding convert—one of the dedicated.

If origami is something new for you it is essential that you begin at the beginning. On no account must you try the difficult folds before you have completed some of the more simple models and begun to understand what the hobby is all about.

This book features a collection of remarkable folds by Patricia Crawford of the United States. Her folds are complex and in some cases quite difficult to do . . . but be assured you can, with a little concentration, get just as good a result as the creator herself.

Origami is not meant to be easy. Origami is a challenge and it is possible that some time will pass before you solve all the problems I have laid before you.

If you are already a keen paper-folder, then you will be very excited when you find just how many new and wonderful folds there are in these pages.

Although I have tried to put as much detail as possible into the illustrations, and provide as many step-by-step drawings as possible, a great deal is left for you to discover from the signs, symbols, and a few helpful words.

Before You Begin

Symbols

The symbols are based on Akira Yoshizawa's code of lines and arrows. The first thing to do is to study and remember the symbols. Once you get these signs and symbols well into your head, following the step-by-step illustrations will be no problem for you.

Each drawing really tells its story. Examine the symbols carefully, and immediately you should know what to do. However, in many cases a few words of explanation have been inserted here and there. These should not be necessary, but may help a beginner.

The symbols are self-explanatory. The little arrows tell you just what to do. One arrow means fold in front, another fold behind, and yet another fold under or into and so on.

Most books on origami adopt a set of symbols very like the ones in this book, and if there are differences you will soon see just what they are.

The first few pages contain several simple folds which will give you as much practice as you need to tackle the more advanced folds.

Try to read the symbols and *see* in your mind just how a fold must be made.

So . . . for ten minutes, study those symbols.

Precreasing

This means that in order to make the model easier to fold, a certain amount of preliminary creasing is necessary. Once these essential creases have been made it is then comparatively simple to arrive at the correct result.

Patricia Crawford's "Bird Bath" is a typical example of detailed precreasing. Once the creases have been made the rest of the folds are fairly simple.

When precreasing, it is necessary to find some guide lines and wherever possible these have been given, so that when the first few folds are made other guide lines are automatically created, and so on until all the folds have been made.

Procedures

In origami there are several standard procedures which you may or may not already know. In the early pages you will notice that certain procedures are shown in detail. For example: on page 11 you will see in Figs. 1 to 10 that flaps are lifted and pressed flat—they are "squashed." This will happen a number of times.

On page 10 you will see how to "sink" two corners, Figs. 24, 25 and 26: how first of all you precrease, then stretch out and "push in." This will happen again several times but not always in the same way: see pages 58–59, Figs. 6, 7, 8 and 9 and so on.

The "Petal-fold" is always being used: see page 9, Figs. 10 to 19. Petal-folds need not always be exactly this shape but the procedure is always the same.

If you come across a written instruction to do this or that or the other and you don't know just what is meant, take a look through the index and see where an example of this fold occurs.

"Reverse-folds" will play a big part in your life. "The Guillemot" is a working example of a series of reverse-folds: inside reverse-folds and outside reverse-folds. In this case precreasing helps, as you will clearly see.

As you work your way through this and other origami books you will become familiar with procedures, and after a while they will become second nature.

Bases

There are many bases: traditional bases and bases created by folders. The Preliminary Base, page 8, the Waterbomb Base, page 12, the Bird Base, page 9, are a few of the many you will come into contact with.

Most creative folders have bases from which they make many folds. Neal Elias and Fred Rohm of the USA are examples of this. Fred Rohm has what he calls his Simplex Base, from which countless folds have been made, especially working models.

In this book you will notice that the "Mermaid," "Christ on the Mount of Olives," and the "Squirrel on the Log" all begin in much the same way.

The Bird Base, the most famous of all traditional bases, has been most used. Then there is the Stretched Bird Base, the Blintzed Bird Base, and so on. Sometimes two bases are mixed together; you will begin to recognize them and probably invent a couple of your own.

Once you are familiar with some of these beginnings you will be able to create your own models. The most popular first creations are some sort of bird, a decorative design, or a box, and then—who knows?—something bigger and better.

So watch out for, and become familiar with, the bases.

Paper

Almost any paper will do, but fine papers make fine models. Do not just tear a piece of paper out of a school notebook and expect to make a neat and attractive model.

If you need a square it must be exactly square; if a triangle or a rectangle the measurements must be exact, otherwise the resulting model will be a monstrosity.

Papers specially made for origami can be found in many shops, and all attractive wrapping papers cut to size are ideal. You will notice that Patricia Crawford uses foils. These metallic papers keep good shape and are in some cases essential for the models described.

THE SYMBOLS–These should be memorized now

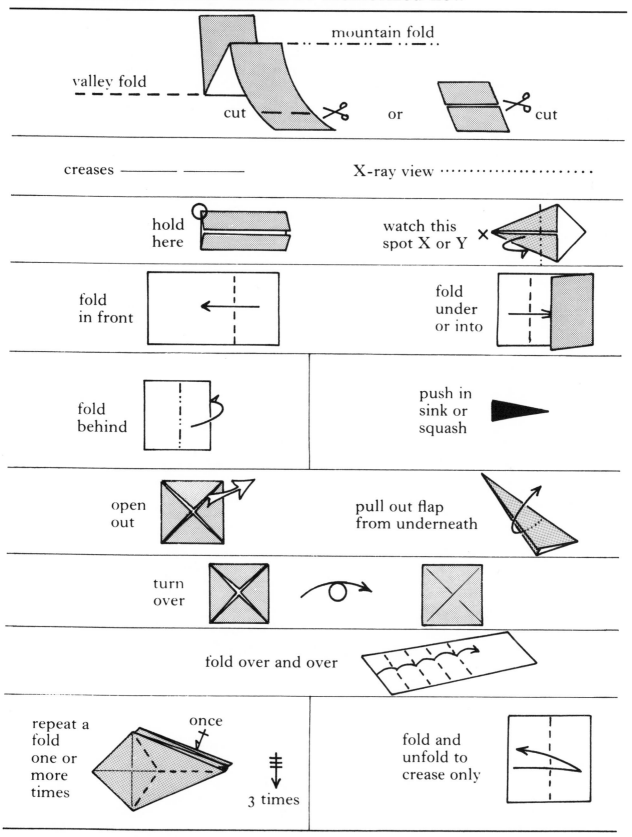

mountain fold

valley fold

cut

or

cut

creases ———— ————

X-ray view ·······················

hold here

watch this spot X or Y

fold in front

fold under or into

fold behind

push in sink or squash

open out

pull out flap from underneath

turn over

fold over and over

repeat a fold one or more times

once

3 times

fold and unfold to crease only

HOW TO USE THE SYMBOLS Making a flower

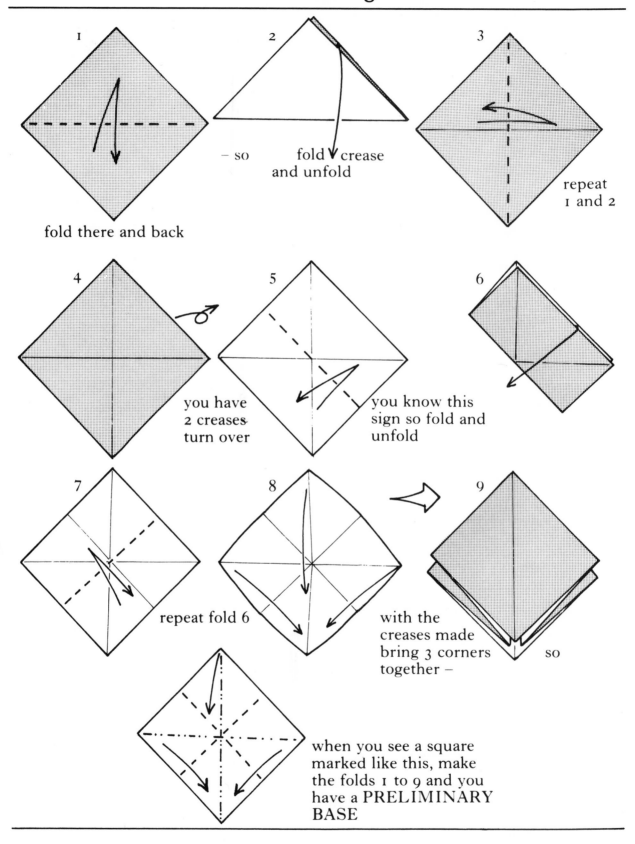

1

fold there and back

2

– so   fold ▾ crease
and unfold

3

repeat
1 and 2

4

you have
2 creases
turn over

5

you know this
sign so fold and
unfold

6

7

repeat fold 6

8

9

with the
creases made
bring 3 corners
together –

so

when you see a square
marked like this, make
the folds 1 to 9 and you
have a PRELIMINARY
BASE

USE OF SYMBOLS Making a flower *(continued)*

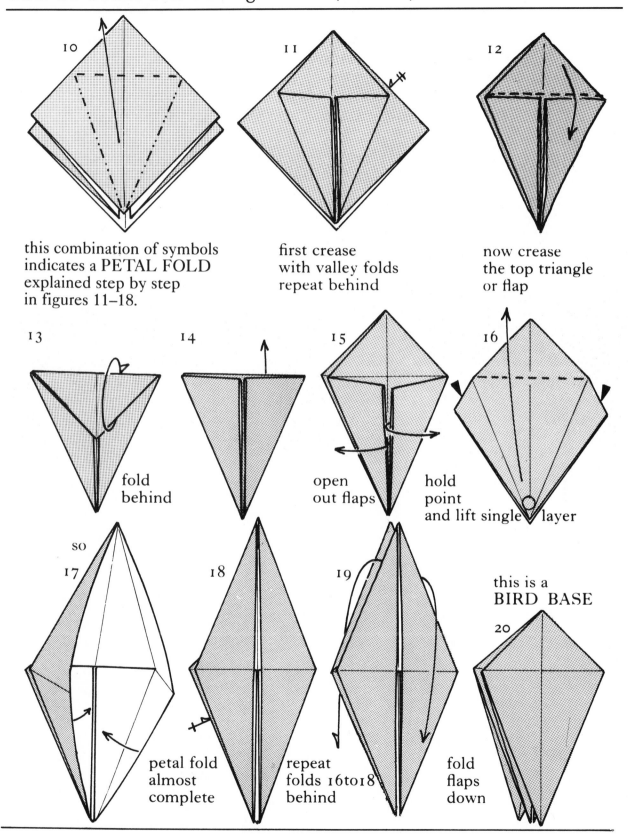

10

this combination of symbols
indicates a PETAL FOLD
explained step by step
in figures 11–18.

11

first crease
with valley folds
repeat behind

12

now crease
the top triangle
or flap

13

fold
behind

14

15

open
out flaps

hold
point
and lift single layer

16

so

17

petal fold
almost
complete

18

repeat
folds 16to18
behind

19

fold
flaps
down

this is a
BIRD BASE

20

Making a flower Philip Shen Hong Kong

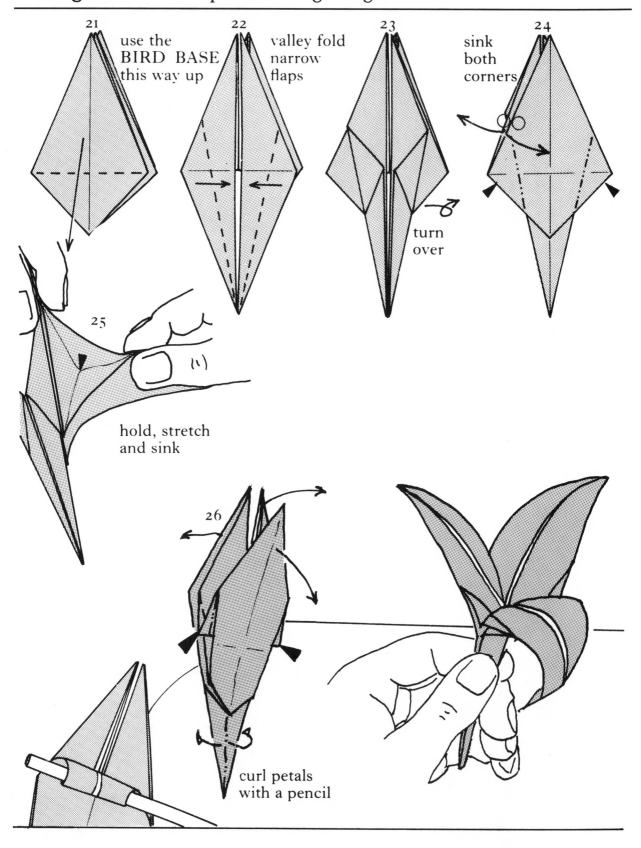

21 use the BIRD BASE this way up

22 valley fold narrow flaps

23 turn over

24 sink both corners

25 hold, stretch and sink

26 curl petals with a pencil

USE OF SYMBOLS Japanese Box

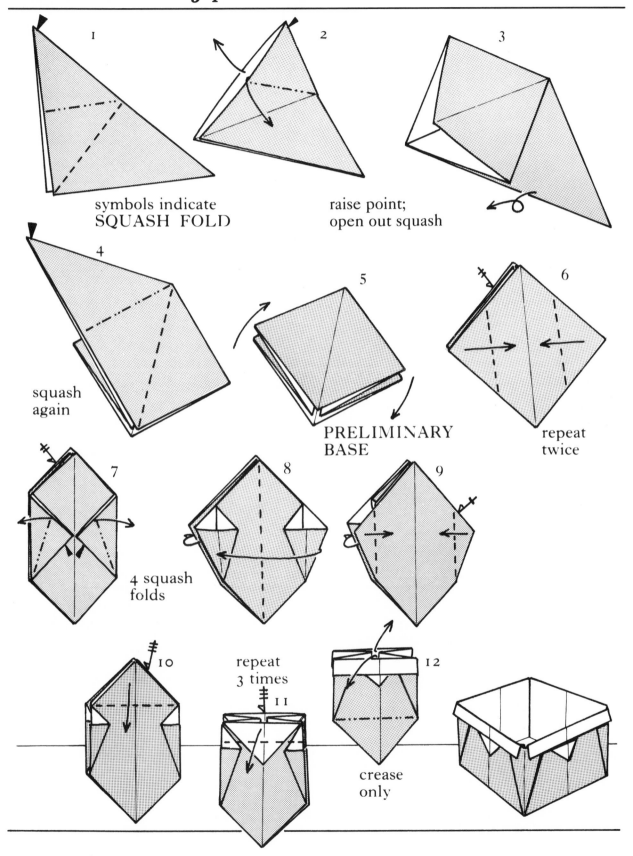

1 symbols indicate
SQUASH FOLD

2 raise point;
open out squash

3

4 squash
again

5 PRELIMINARY
BASE

6 repeat
twice

7 4 squash
folds

8

9

10

repeat
3 times

11

12 crease
only

USE OF SYMBOLS Waterbomb Base

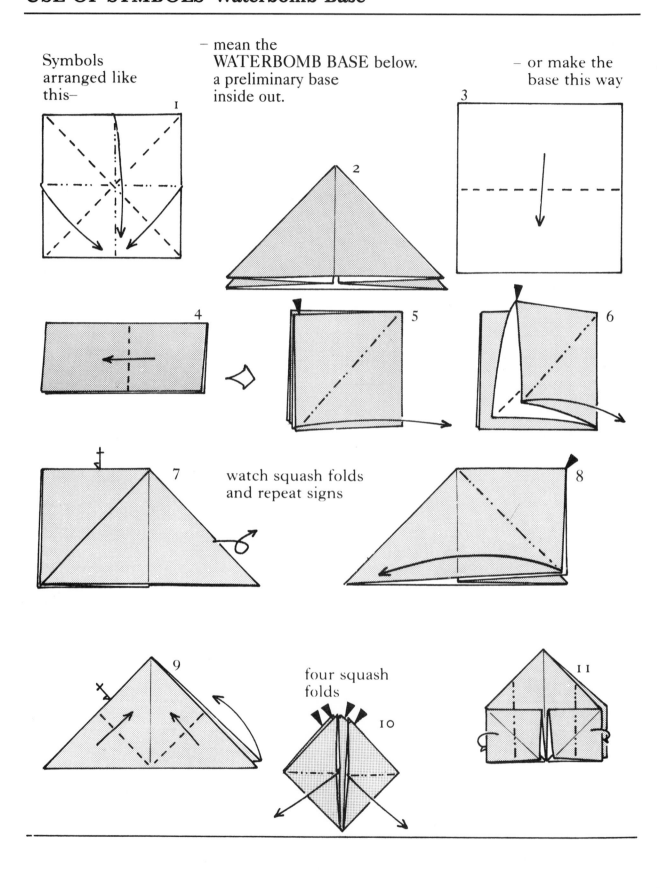

Symbols arranged like this–

– mean the WATERBOMB BASE below. a preliminary base inside out.

– or make the base this way

watch squash folds and repeat signs

four squash folds

USE OF SYMBOLS Church and Fancy Box

The waterbomb base is the starting point for
endless models. Here are two.

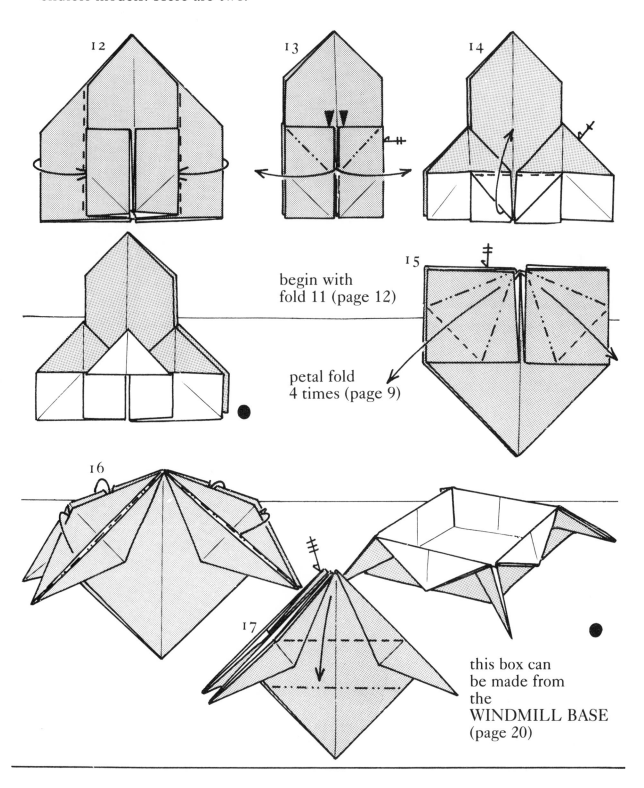

begin with
fold 11 (page 12)

petal fold
4 times (page 9)

this box can
be made from
the
WINDMILL BASE
(page 20)

Lover's Knot–Traditional *An exercise*

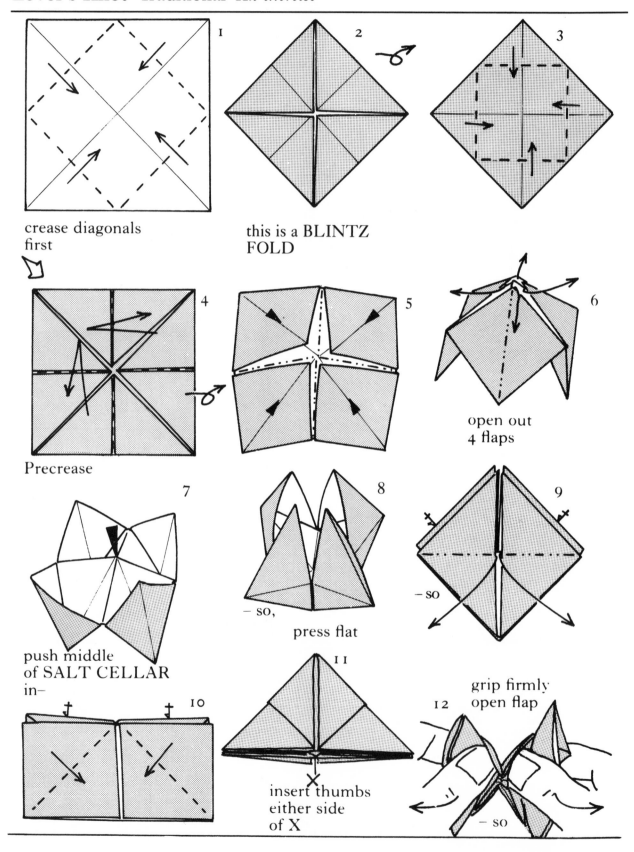

1 crease diagonals first

2 this is a BLINTZ FOLD

3

4 Precrease

5

6 open out 4 flaps

7 push middle of SALT CELLAR in–

8 – so, press flat

9 – so

10

11 insert thumbs either side of X

12 grip firmly open flap – so

Lover's Knot *(continued)*

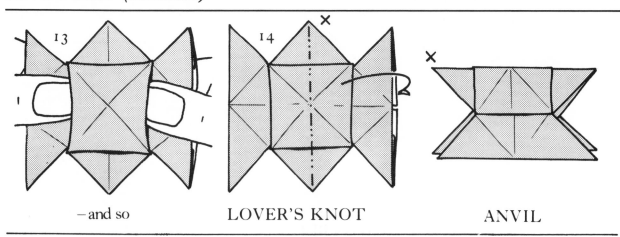

— and so   LOVER'S KNOT   ANVIL

Super-Box John Richardson Gt. Britain

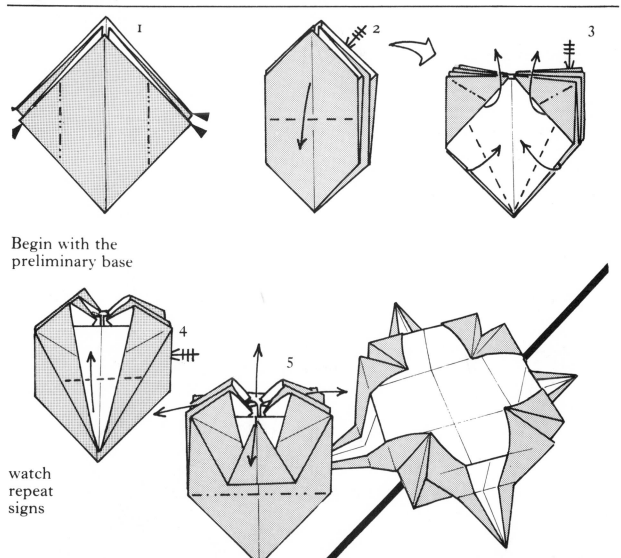

Begin with the
preliminary base

watch
repeat
signs

Guillemot Robert Harbin Gt. Britain

Use a square
black on one side.
Follow the symbols.

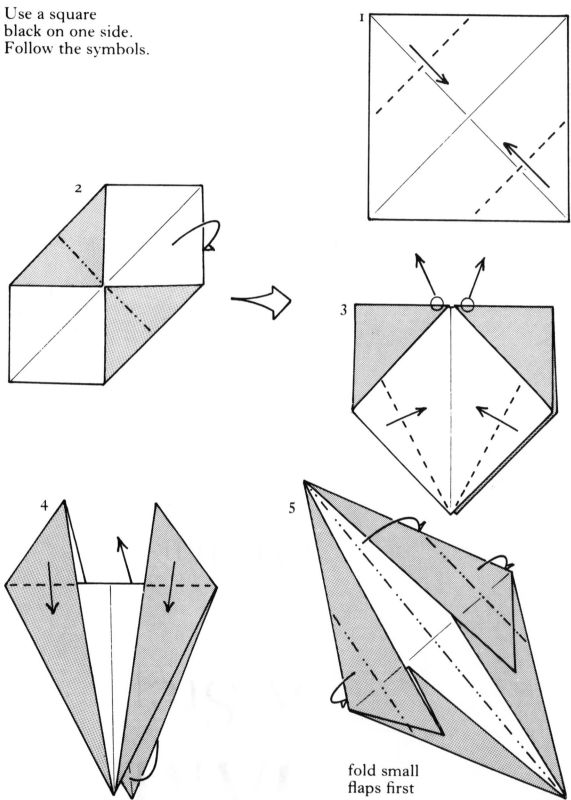

fold small
flaps first

Guillemot *(continued)*

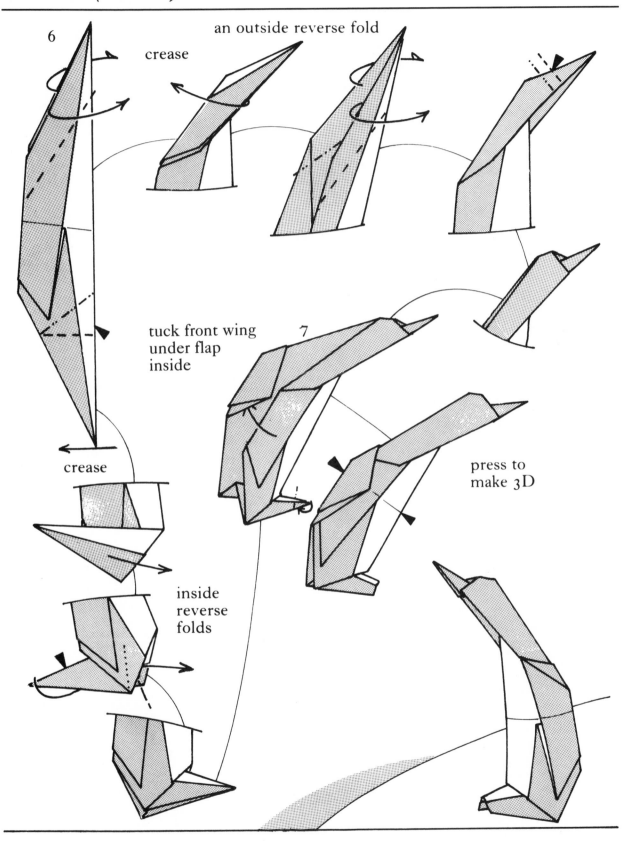

6

crease

an outside reverse fold

tuck front wing
under flap
inside

7

press to
make 3D

crease

inside
reverse
folds

Tetrahedron (Geometric solid) Patricia Crawford U.S.A.

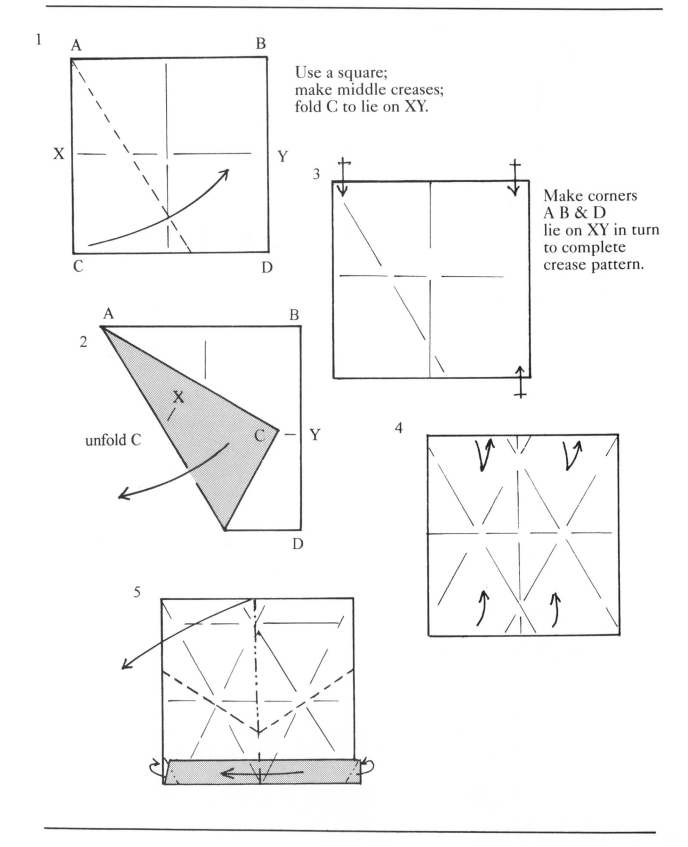

1

A   B

X   Y

C   D

Use a square;
make middle creases;
fold C to lie on XY.

3

Make corners
A B & D
lie on XY in turn
to complete
crease pattern.

2

A   B

unfold C

C   Y

D

4

5

Tetrahedron *(continued)*

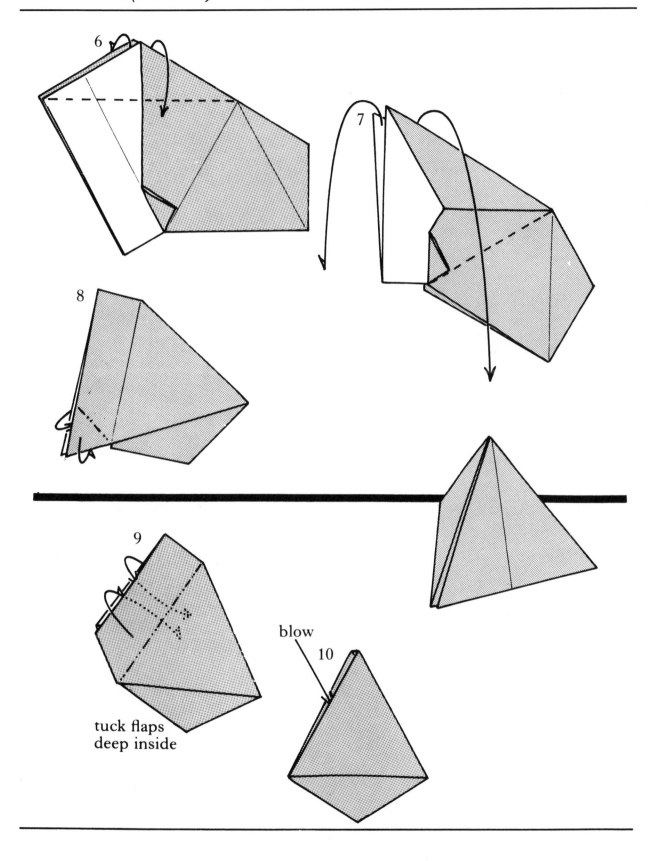

tuck flaps
deep inside

blow

Decoration Folding exercise Japan

Use a square, either side up. Creases 1 to 5 produce 7.
Squash folds produce 8, the Windmill Base. With this base
endless decorative folds can be devised. 8 squash folds are used (fig. 10).

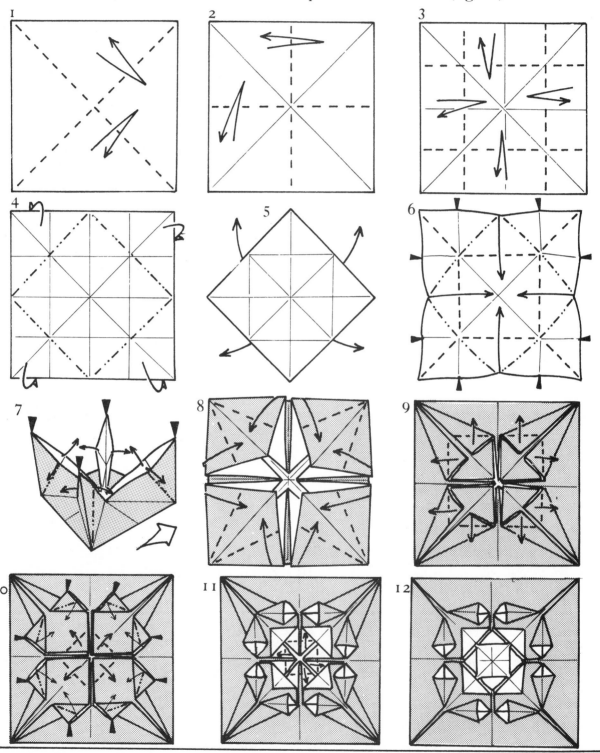

Yacht Toshie Takahama Japan

An example of this woman's genius.
Five simple folds make a yacht.

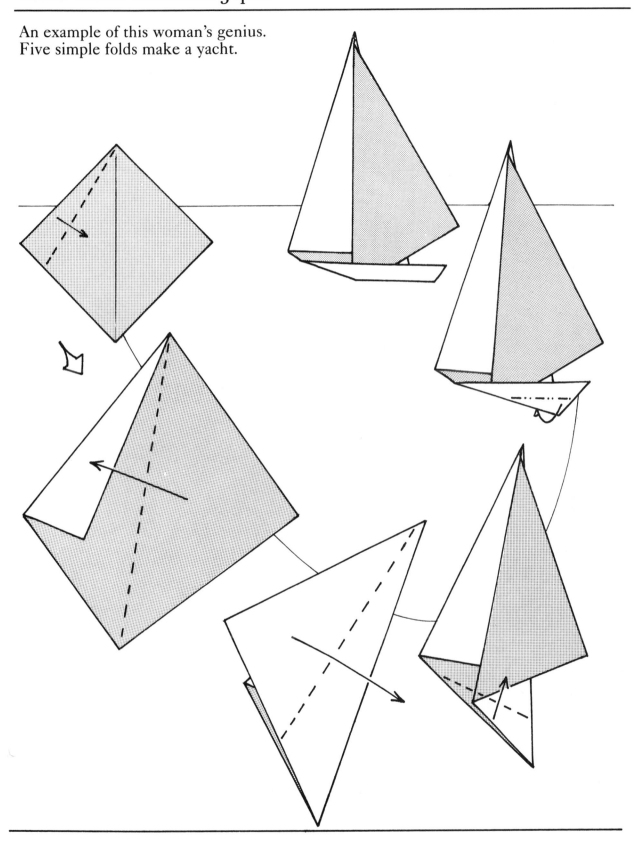

Speedboat Ian Archer *(age 13)* Gt. Britain

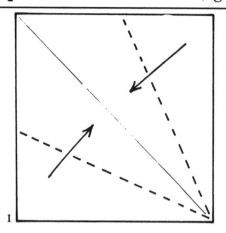

For this outboard motor craft, crease a square along diagonal and fold in sides.

In 5 crease the long narrow flaps

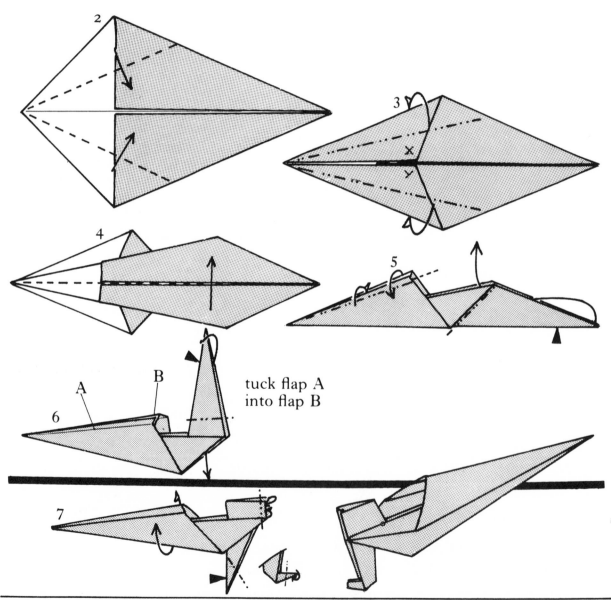

tuck flap A into flap B

Simple Dart John Smith Gt. Britain

An exercise in folding – mostly valley folds.

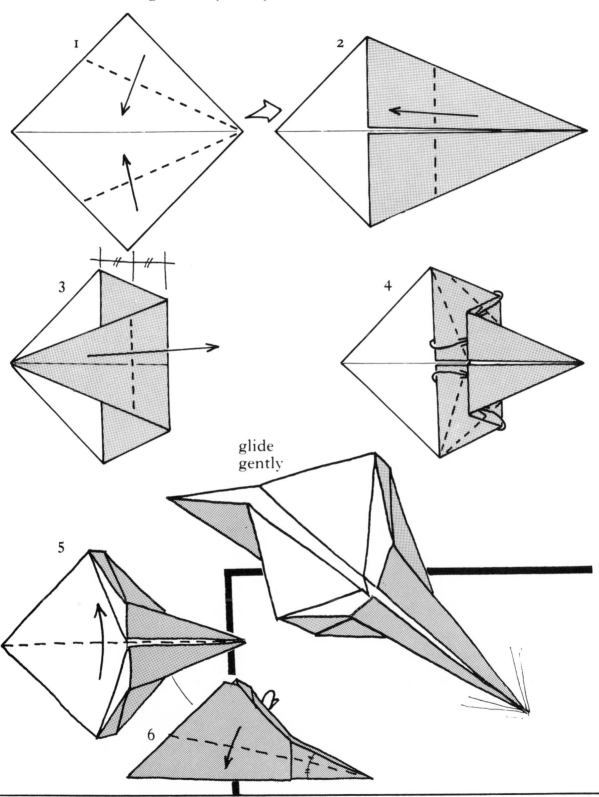

glide
gently

Lakotoi *(New Guinea)* Philip Noble Scotland

Use a square of very thin white paper for this authentic model.

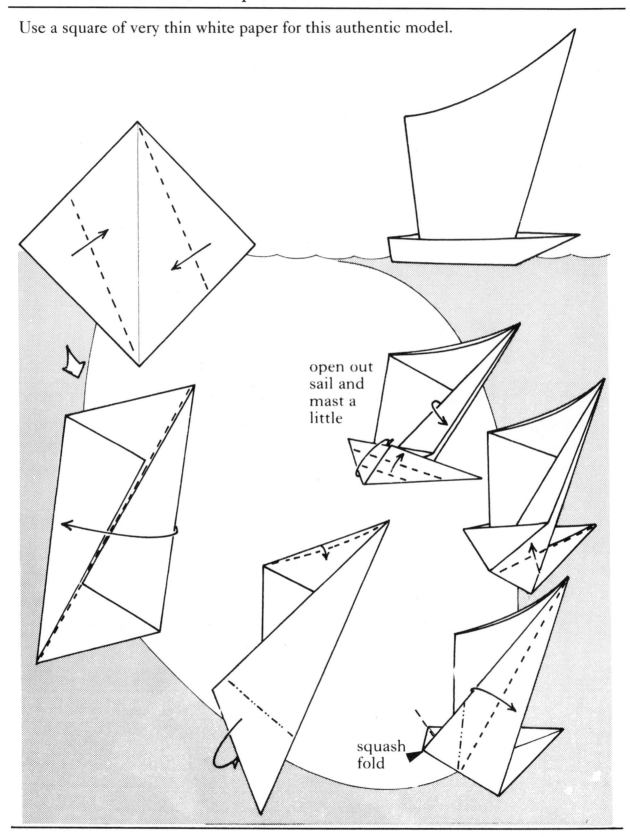

open out
sail and
mast a
little

squash
fold

"No Walk Today" Philip Noble Scotland

Use a square of paper, brown
on one side. Fold in half.
Varied adjustments of the second fold
produce different dogs and pups.

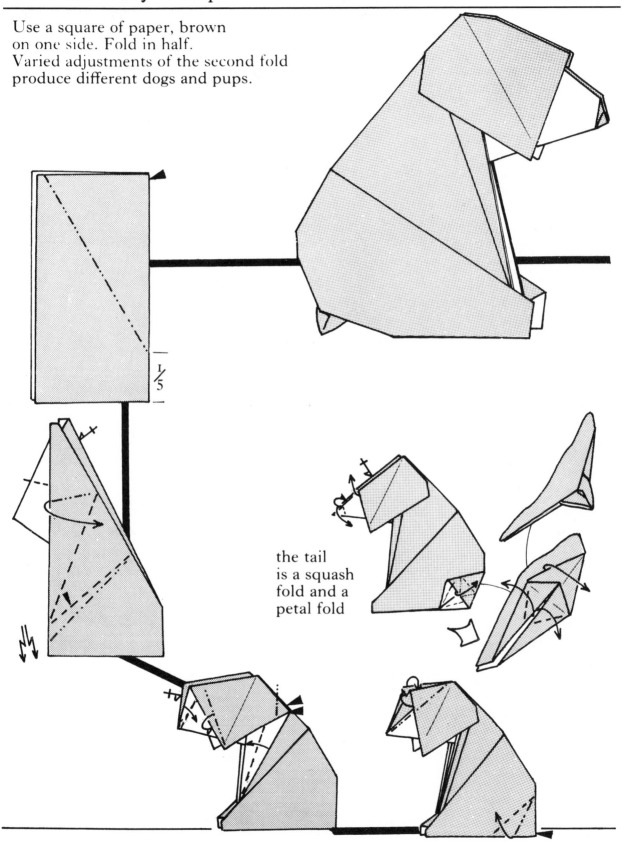

the tail
is a squash
fold and a
petal fold

$\frac{1}{5}$

Two Nuns Robert Harbin Gt. Britain

Use a square of paper,
black on one side.
Crease diagonals and
fold 3 corners to the center.

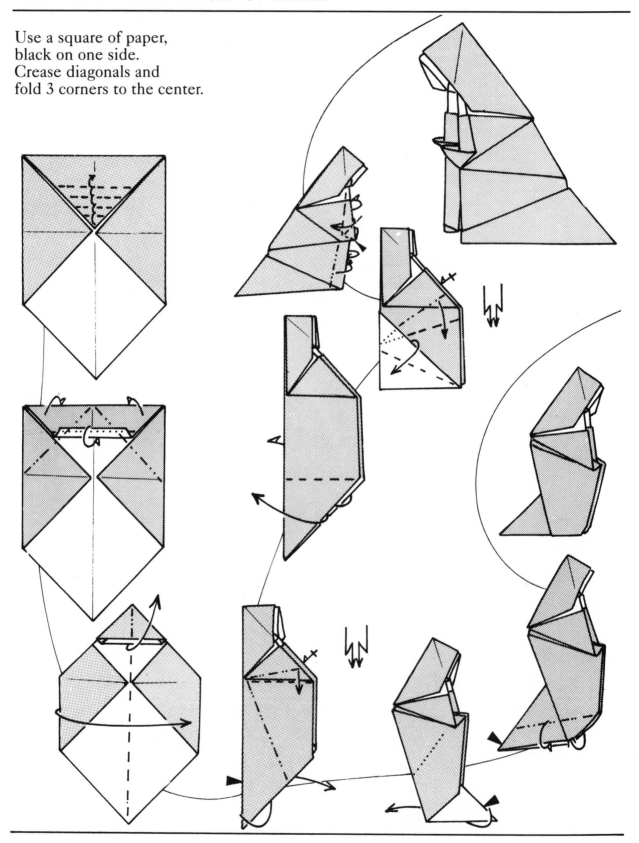

The Film Star Eric Kenneway Gt. Britain

Use a square of paper, yellow on one side.
Make center creases as a guide.

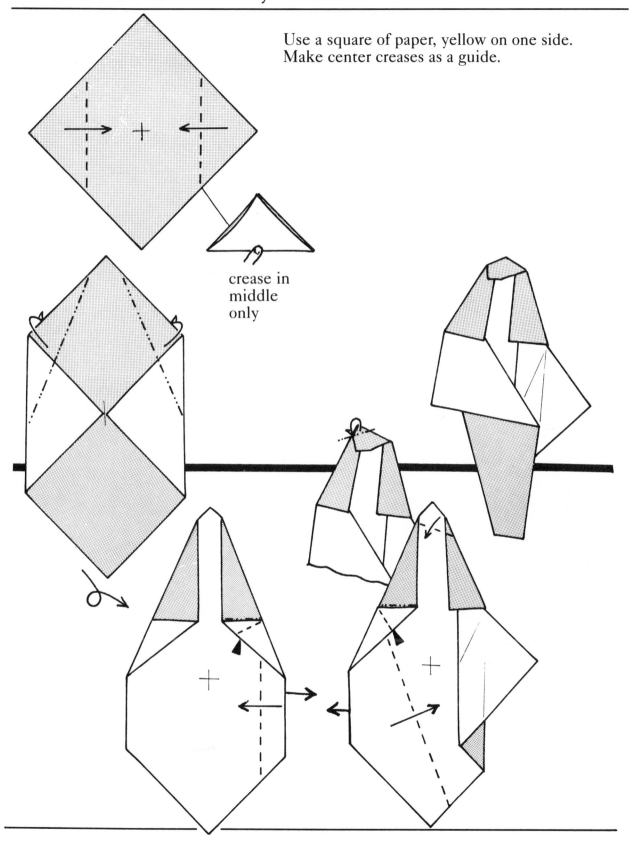

crease in
middle
only

Octahedron (Geometric solid) Patricia Crawford U.S.A.

Use a square of paper.
Crease the diagonals,
fold in half, then fold
points right then left.

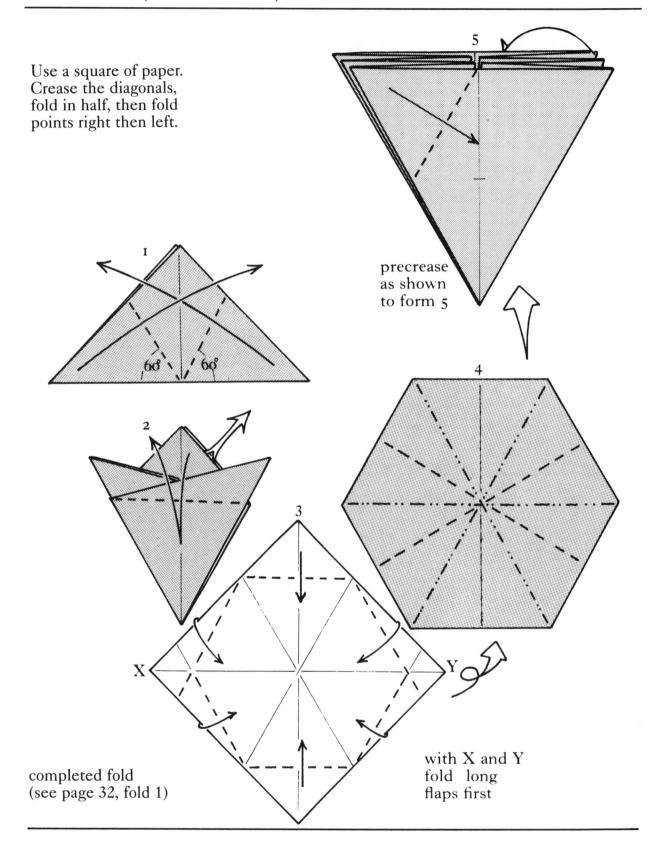

precrease
as shown
to form 5

with X and Y
fold long
flaps first

completed fold
(see page 32, fold 1)

Octahedron *(continued)*

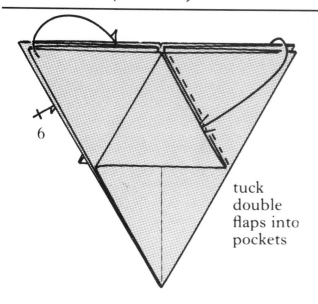

6

tuck
double
flaps into
pockets

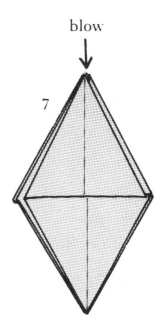

blow

7

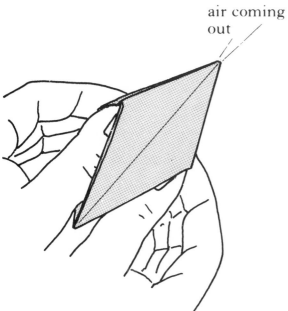

air coming
out

put thumbs
into pockets
to make bellows

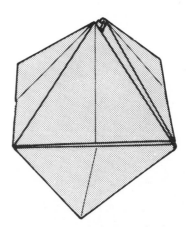

Stalking Cat Patricia Crawford U.S.A.

Use a square of foil white side down.
Crease diagonals and fold corners as indicated.

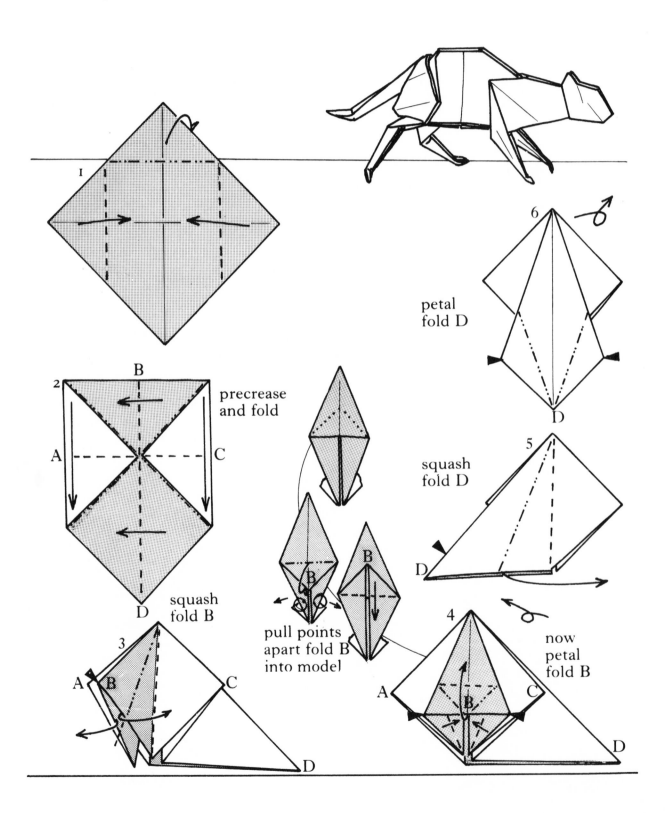

I

6

petal
fold D

D

2

B

precrease
and fold

A   C

D

squash
fold B

squash
fold D

D

5

pull points
apart fold B
into model

B

B

3

A   B   C

D

4

now
petal
fold B

A   B   C

D

Stalking Cat *(continued) Just concentrate . . .*

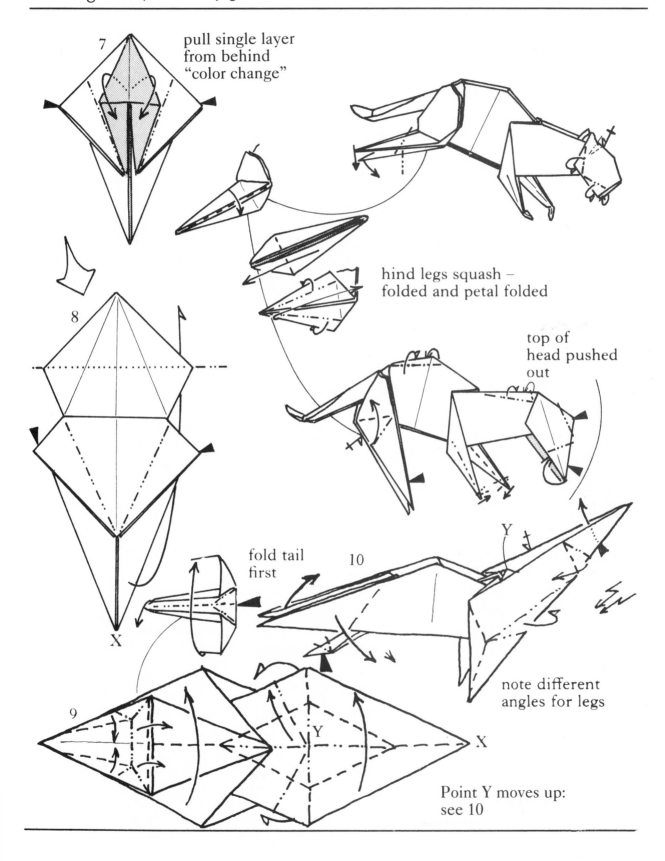

7 pull single layer
from behind
"color change"

hind legs squash –
folded and petal folded

top of
head pushed
out

8

fold tail
first

10

note different
angles for legs

9

Point Y moves up:
see 10

X

Y

X

Y

Birdbath Patricia Crawford U.S.A.

Use a colored square of foil (6in. × 6in. or 15cm. × 15cm.). Begin with folds 1, 2 and 3 (page 28) color side inwards.
Unfold two corners and precrease exactly as indicated.

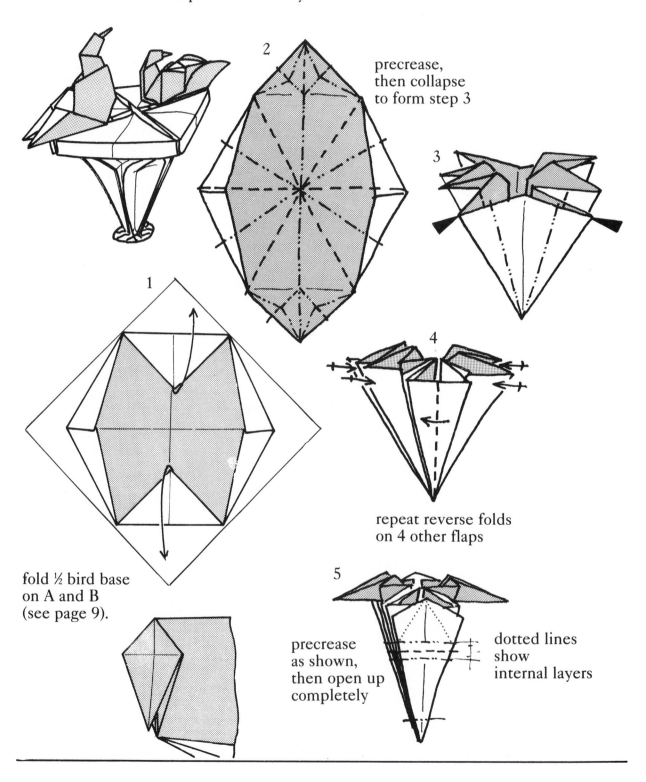

2 precrease, then collapse to form step 3

3

4

repeat reverse folds on 4 other flaps

1

fold ½ bird base on A and B (see page 9).

5

precrease as shown, then open up completely

dotted lines show internal layers

Birdbath *(continued)*

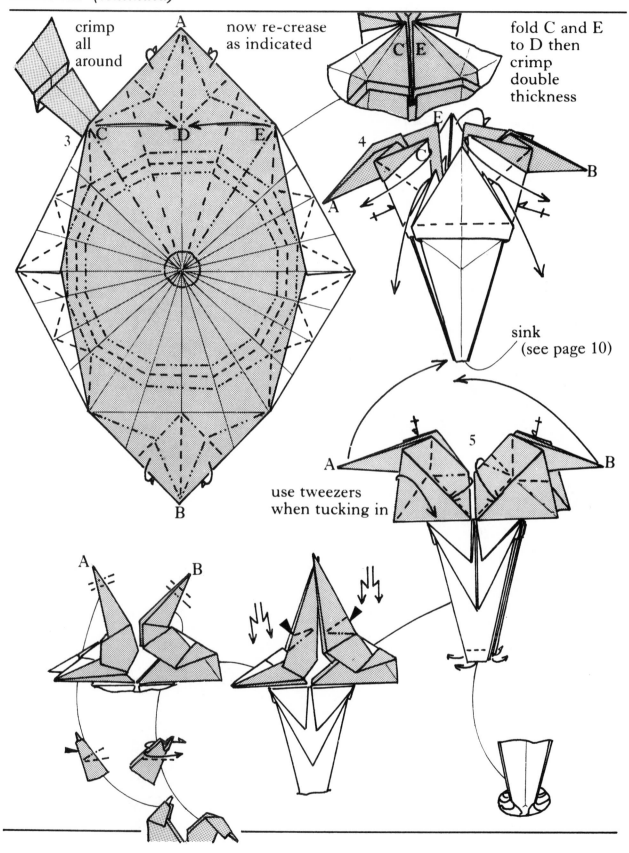

crimp
all
around

now re-crease
as indicated

fold C and E
to D then
crimp
double
thickness

sink
(see page 10)

use tweezers
when tucking in

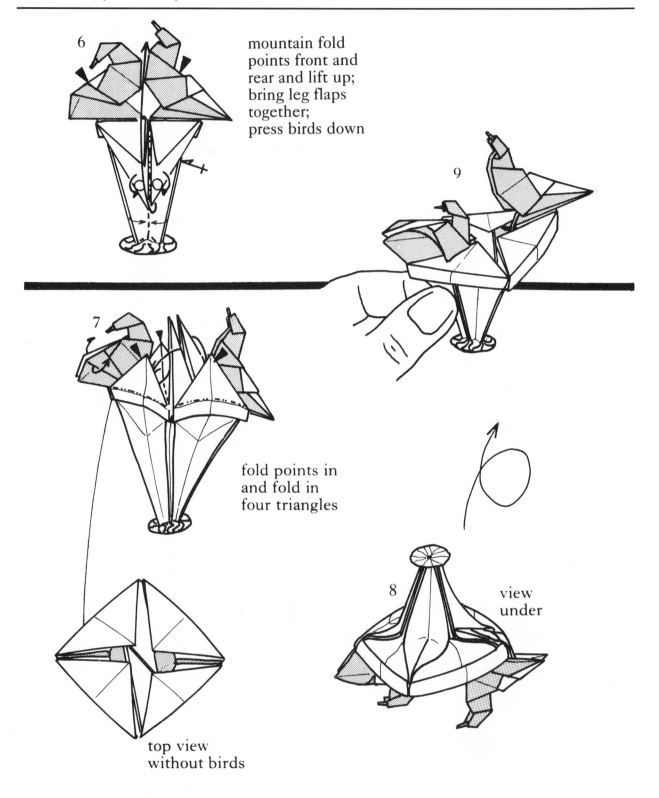

6 mountain fold
points front and
rear and lift up;
bring leg flaps
together;
press birds down

9

7 fold points in
and fold in
four triangles

8 view
under

top view
without birds

Squirrel on a Log Patricia Crawford U.S.A.

Use a square of foil, gold
or log-like on one side

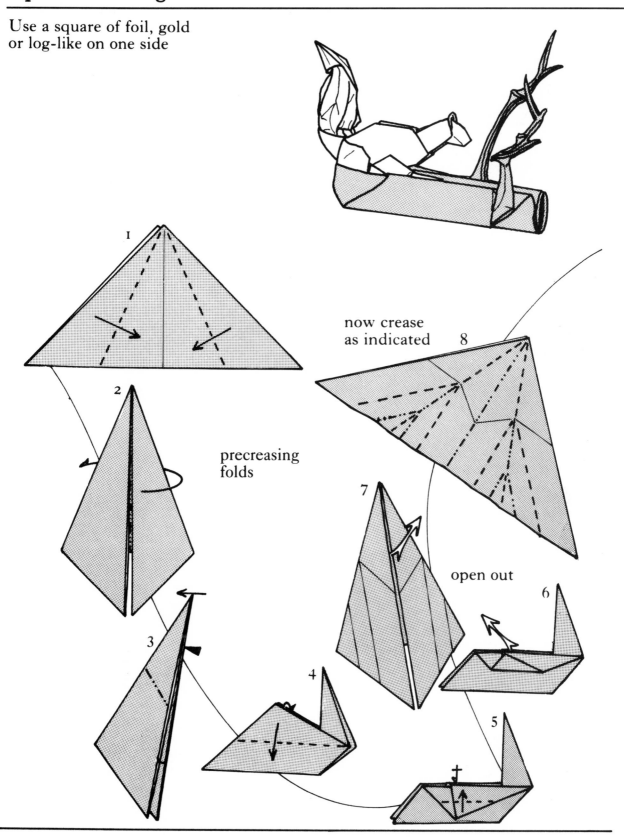

1

2

precreasing
folds

3

4

5

6

7

open out

8

now crease
as indicated

Squirrel on a Log *(continued)*

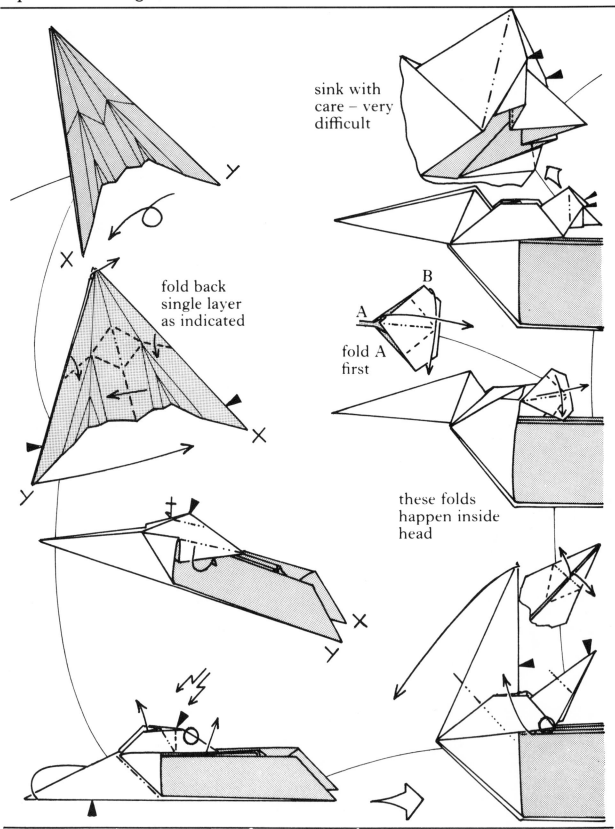

sink with
care – very
difficult

fold back
single layer
as indicated

B

A

fold A
first

these folds
happen inside
head

Squirrel on a Log *(continued)* ... *watch the sink symbols*

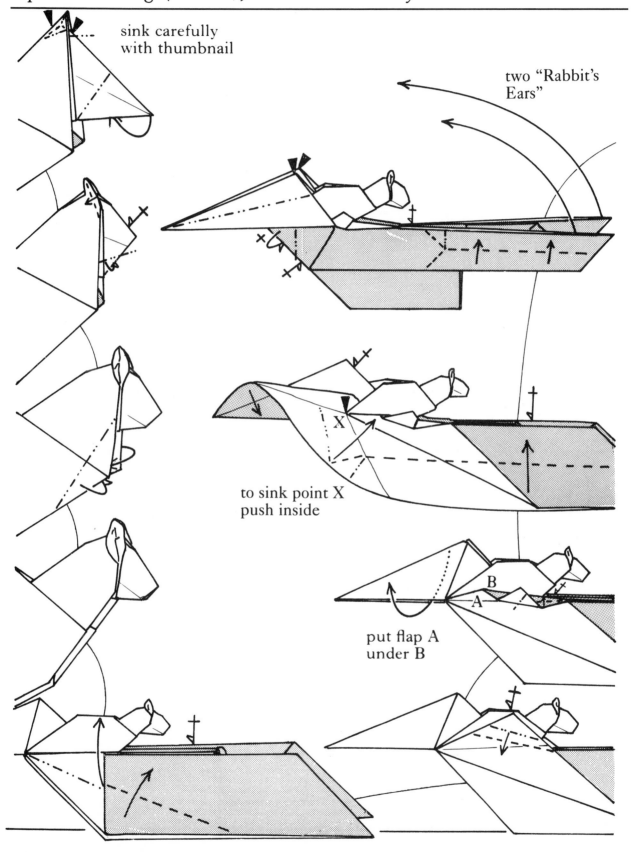

sink carefully
with thumbnail

two "Rabbit's
Ears"

to sink point X
push inside

put flap A
under B

Squirrel on a Log *(continued)*

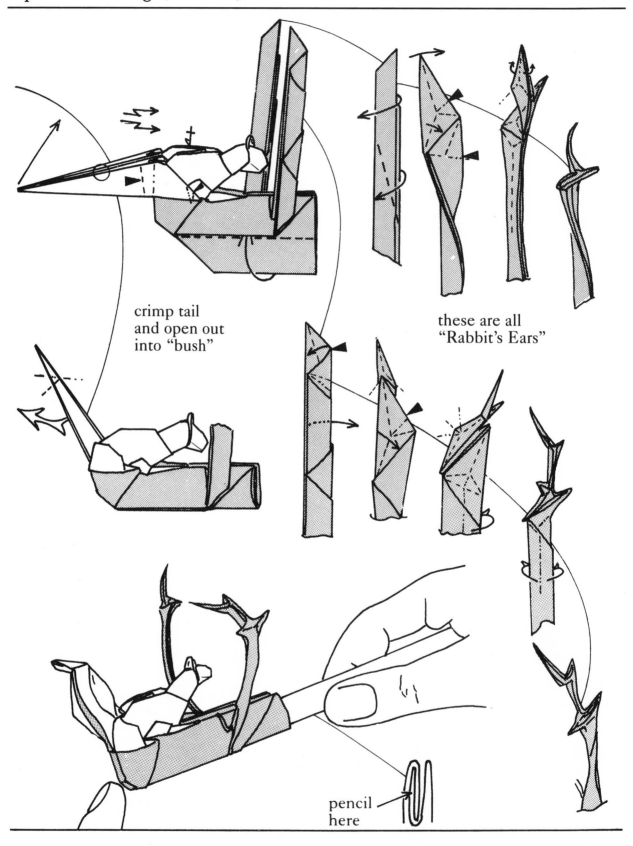

crimp tail
and open out
into "bush"

these are all
"Rabbit's Ears"

pencil
here

Birds in a Nest Patricia Crawford U.S.A.

2 × 3 rectangle brown, gold or nestlike on one side.
Foil works well here. Fold very accurately for the best
results.

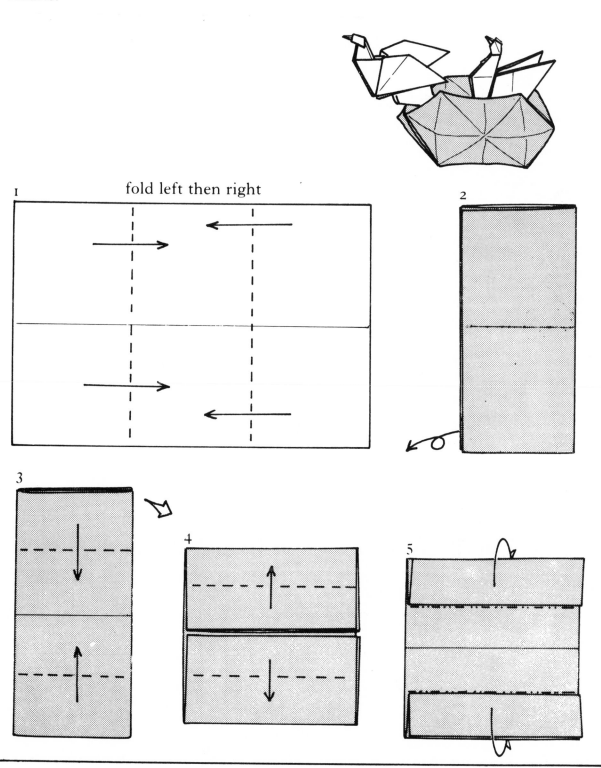

fold left then right

Birds in a Nest *(continued)* . . . *firm creases, please*

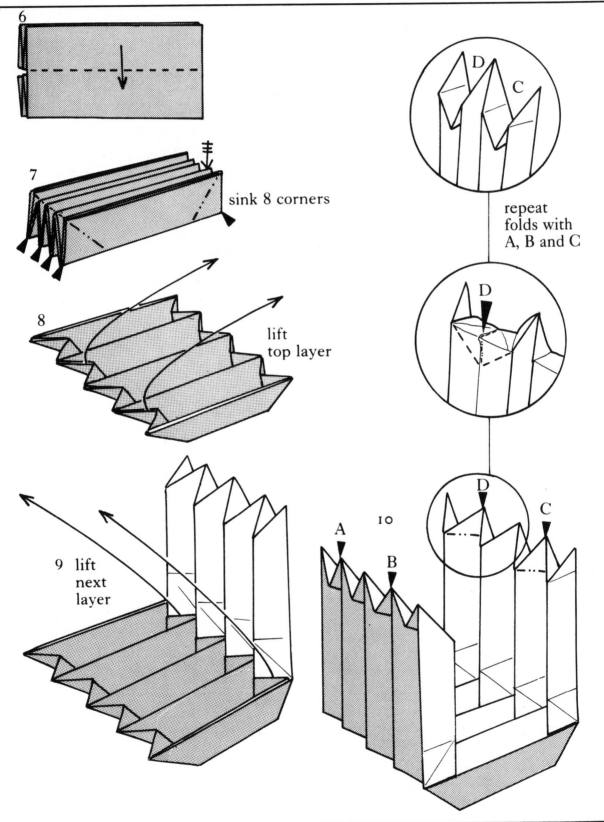

6

7 sink 8 corners

8 lift top layer

9 lift next layer

D C

repeat folds with A, B and C

D

A 10 D C

B

Birds in a Nest *(continued)*

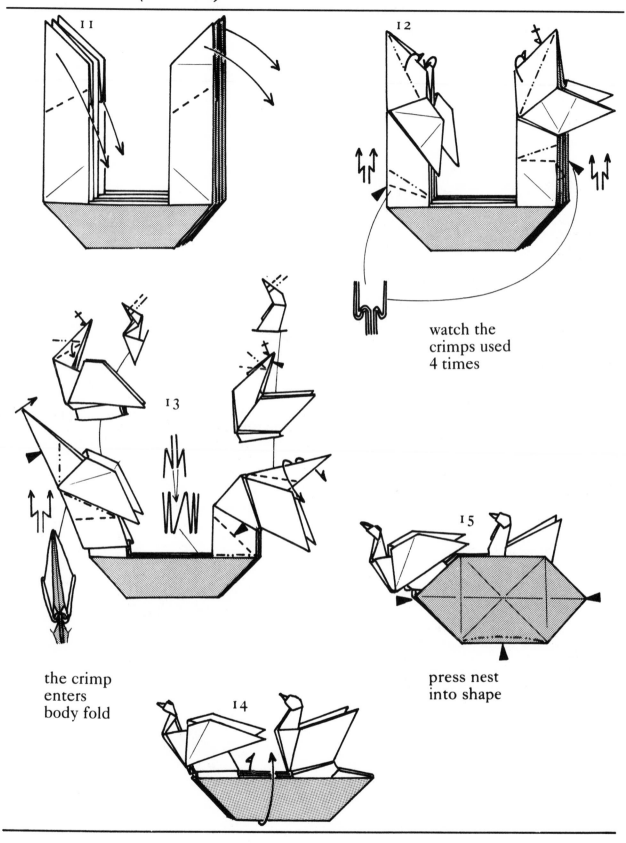

11

12

watch the
crimps used
4 times

13

the crimp
enters
body fold

14

15

press nest
into shape

Mermaid Patricia Crawford U.S.A.

A square of foil, seaweed green on one side.
Similar preparation to squirrel fold.

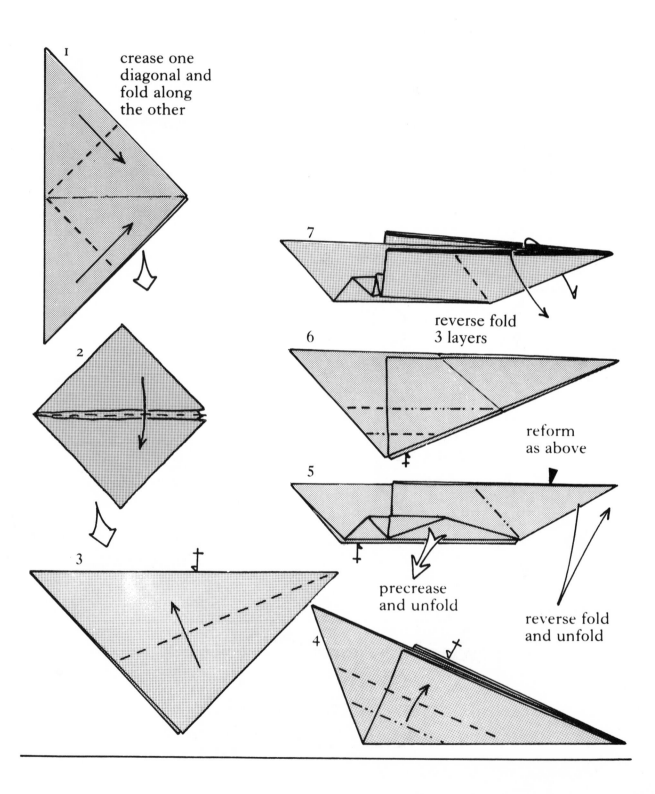

1 crease one diagonal and fold along the other

2

3

4 reverse fold and unfold

5 precrease and unfold

6 reform as above

7 reverse fold 3 layers

Mermaid *(continued) . . . very difficult folds ahead*

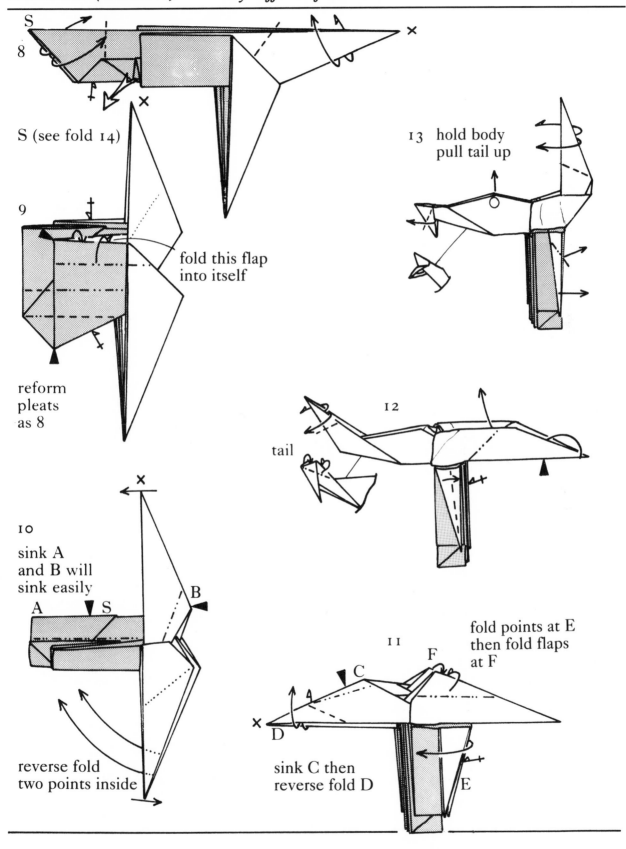

S

8

S (see fold 14)

9

fold this flap
into itself

reform
pleats
as 8

13 hold body
pull tail up

12

tail

10

sink A
and B will
sink easily

A   S   B

reverse fold
two points inside

11

C

F

fold points at E
then fold flaps
at F

D

sink C then
reverse fold D

E

Mermaid *(continued)*

14

pull out S
(see folds 8, 9
and 10)

round the body
by squeezing and
open out seaweed
as indicated

Christ on the Mount of Olives Patricia Crawford U.S.A.

Use a square of foil.
Begin fold 8 of the Mermaid (page 43).
Note slight alteration in 1.

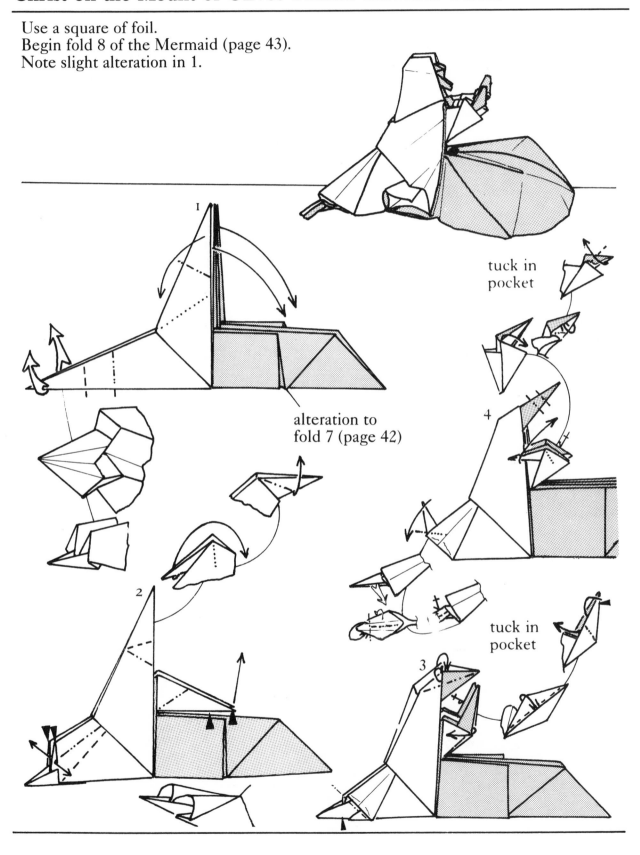

tuck in
pocket

alteration to
fold 7 (page 42)

tuck in
pocket

Christ on the Mount of Olives *(continued)*

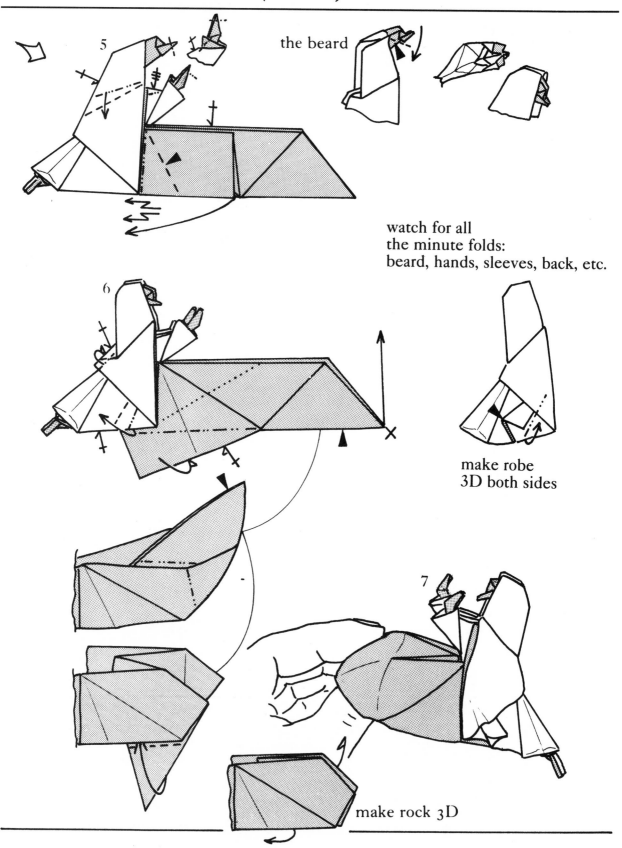

the beard

watch for all
the minute folds:
beard, hands, sleeves, back, etc.

make robe
3D both sides

make rock 3D

Swan Patricia Crawford U.S.A.

Begin with a BIRD BASE
(page 9, fold 20).
Stretch the base
both ways to precrease
large thin white square.

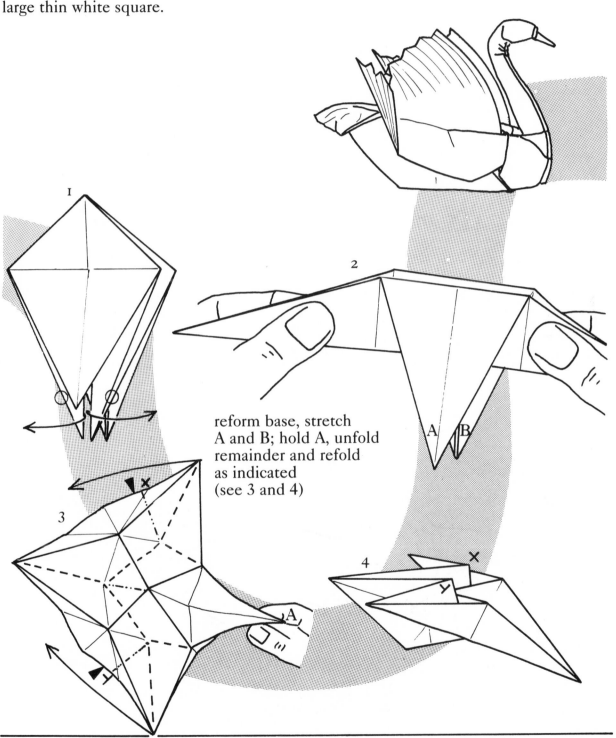

reform base, stretch
A and B; hold A, unfold
remainder and refold
as indicated
(see 3 and 4)

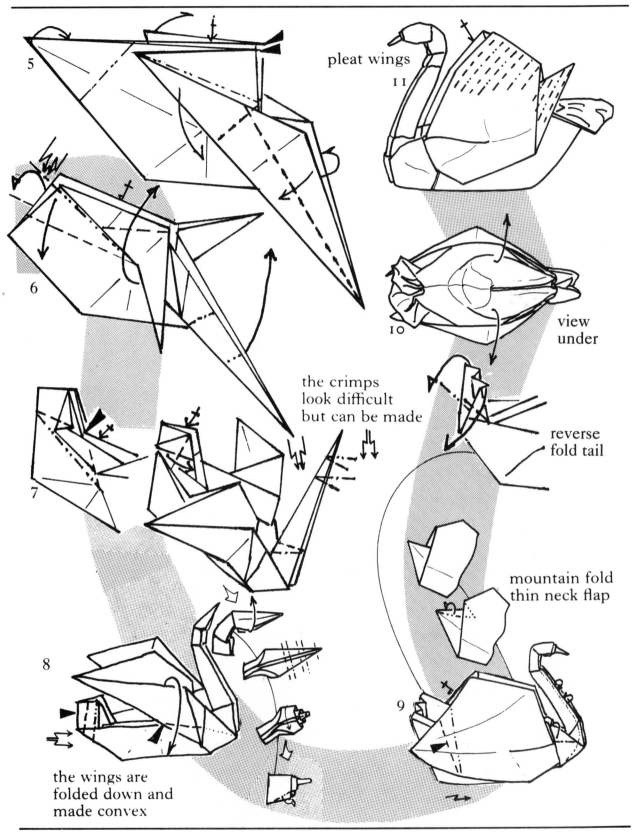

5

6

7

8

the wings are
folded down and
made convex

pleat wings

11

10

view
under

the crimps
look difficult
but can be made

reverse
fold tail

mountain fold
thin neck flap

9

Unicorn Patricia Crawford U.S.A.

Use a square of foil. Begin with
fold 2 of the Mermaid (page 42).

1

2

2 "Rabbit's Ears"

7

reverse fold
hidden points

6

Bird Base
(see page 9)
hold and stretch

× 3

squash fold
(see page 11)

5

4

thick side

Unicorn *(continued)*

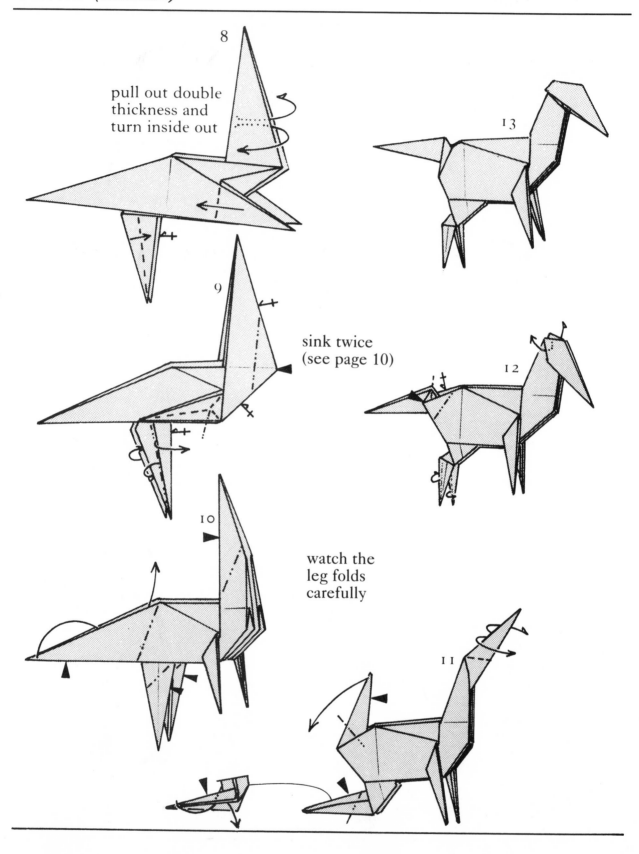

8

pull out double
thickness and
turn inside out

9

sink twice
(see page 10)

13

12

10

watch the
leg folds
carefully

11

Unicorn *(continued)*

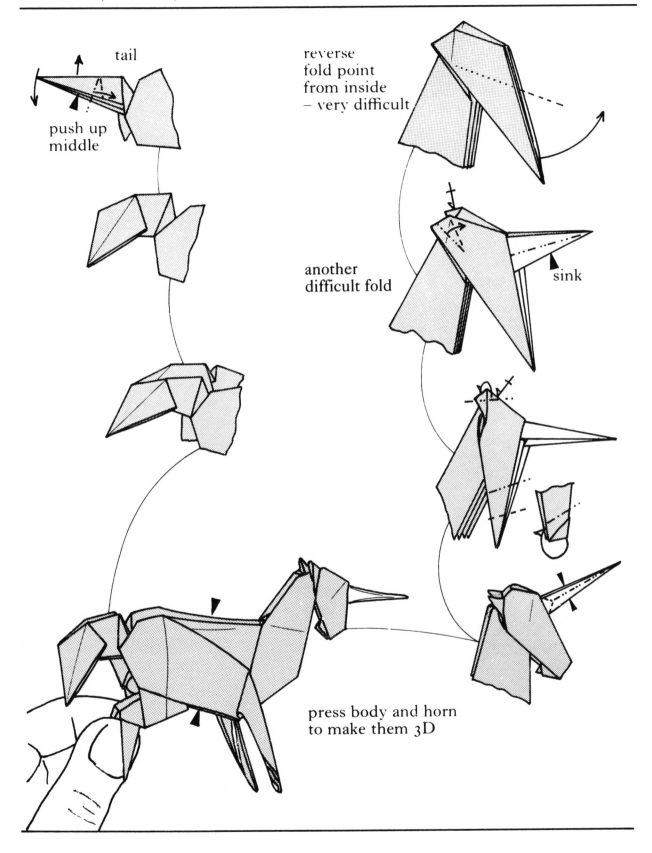

tail

push up
middle

reverse
fold point
from inside
– very difficult

another
difficult fold

sink

press body and horn
to make them 3D

Kangaroo Patricia Crawford U.S.A.

Crease a square in the center only and valley fold 3 corners.
Then turn over and carefully precrease as indicated.

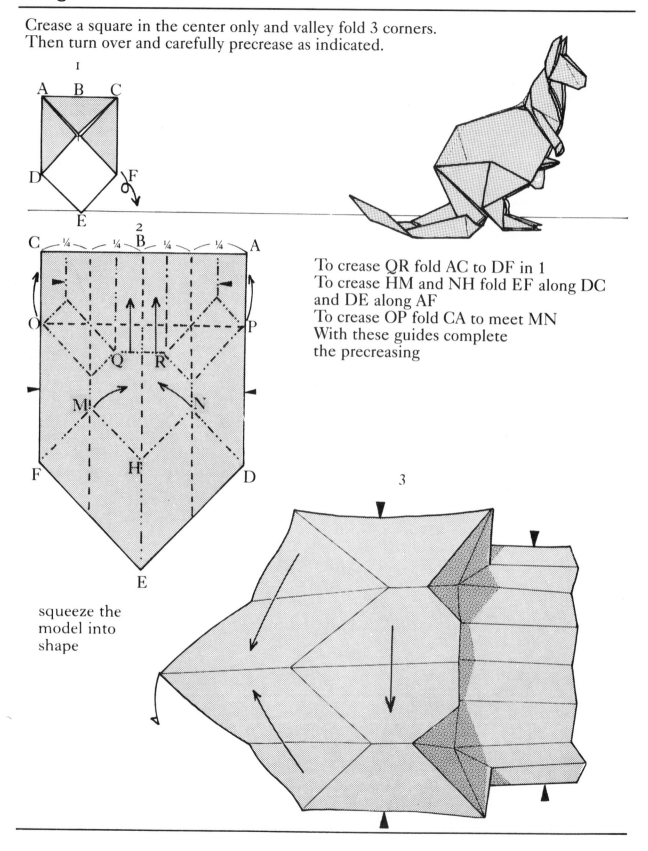

To crease QR fold AC to DF in 1
To crease HM and NH fold EF along DC
and DE along AF
To crease OP fold CA to meet MN
With these guides complete
the precreasing

squeeze the
model into
shape

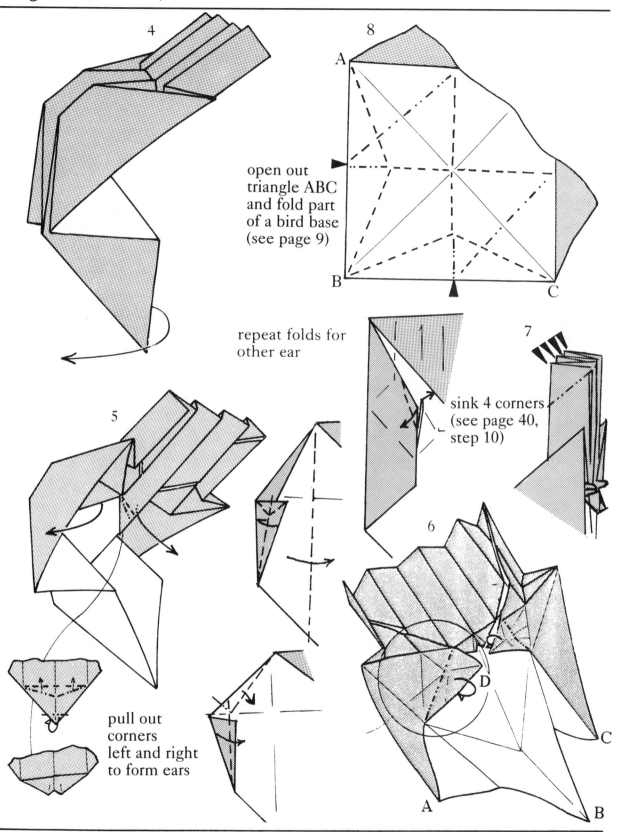

4

8

A

B

C

open out
triangle ABC
and fold part
of a bird base
(see page 9)

repeat folds for
other ear

sink 4 corners
(see page 40,
step 10)

7

5

6

D

C

pull out
corners
left and right
to form ears

A

B

Kangaroo *(continued)*

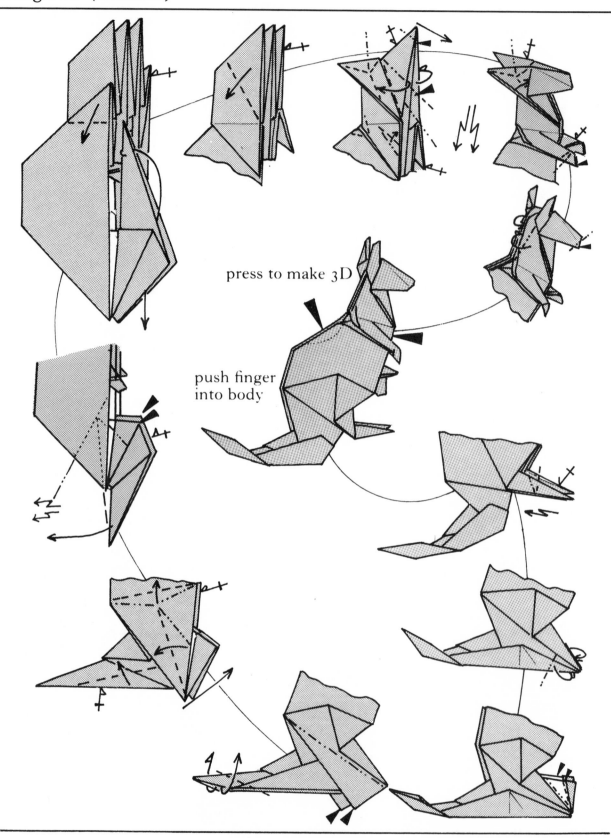

press to make 3D

push finger
into body

Scorpion Patricia Crawford U.S.A.

Use a dark green square of foil.
Begin with a PRELIMINARY BASE.
(see page 8, fold 9)

1

squash 4 corners
form frog base

6

2

petal fold

push sides in

3

4

5

Scorpion *(continued)*

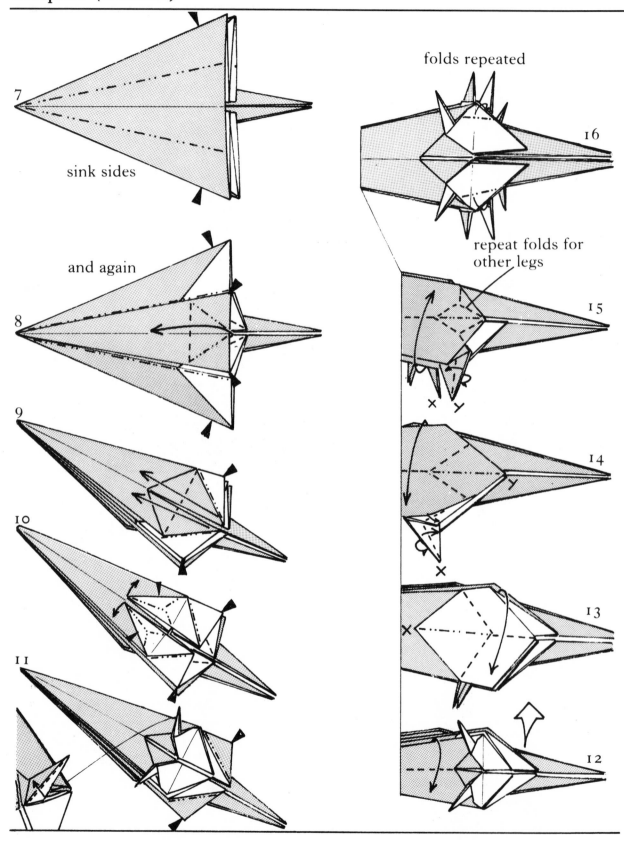

7 sink sides

and again

8

9

10

11

12

13

14

15

repeat folds for other legs

16

folds repeated

Scorpion *(continued)*

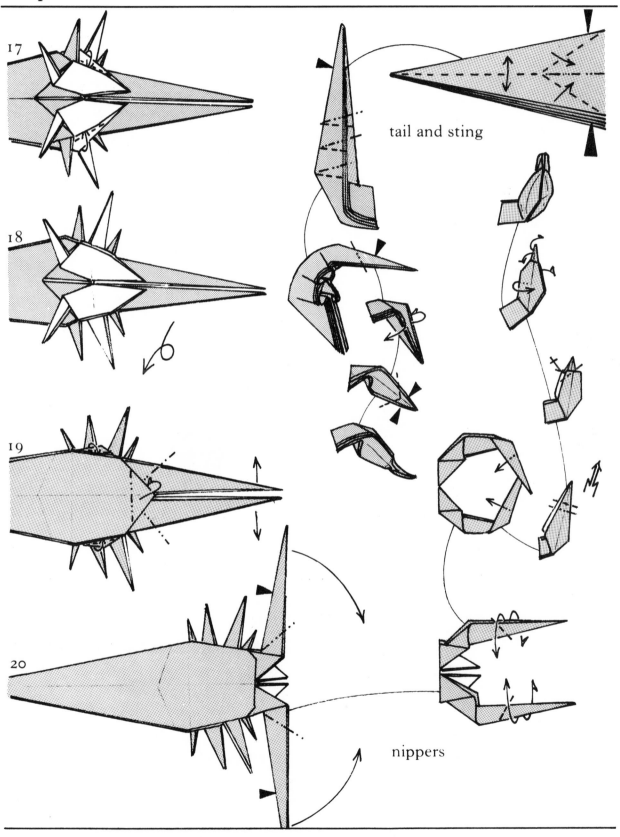

17

18

19

20

tail and sting

nippers

Full-rigged Ship Patricia Crawford U.S.A.

Use a square of red foil.
Begin with a BIRD BASE (see page 9).

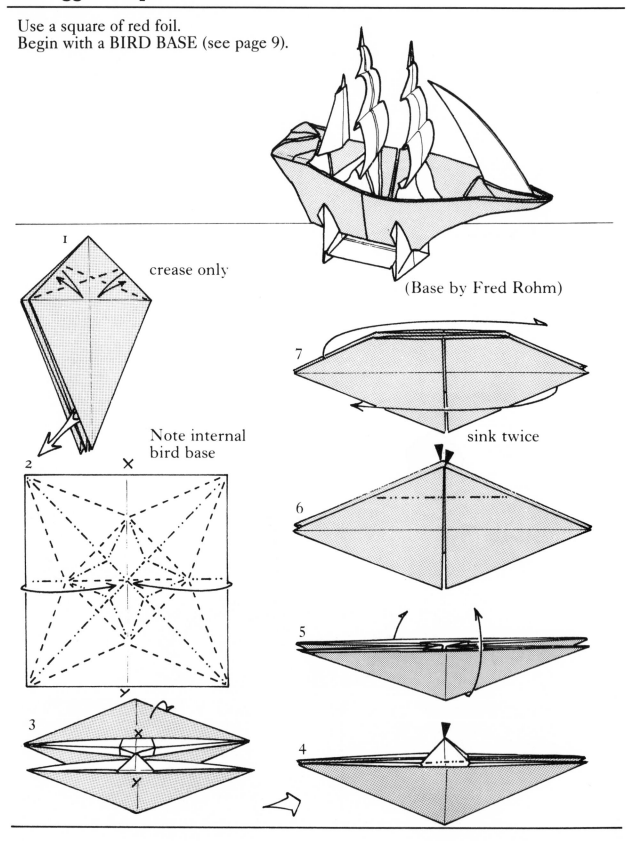

crease only

(Base by Fred Rohm)

Note internal
bird base

sink twice

Full-rigged Ship *(continued)*

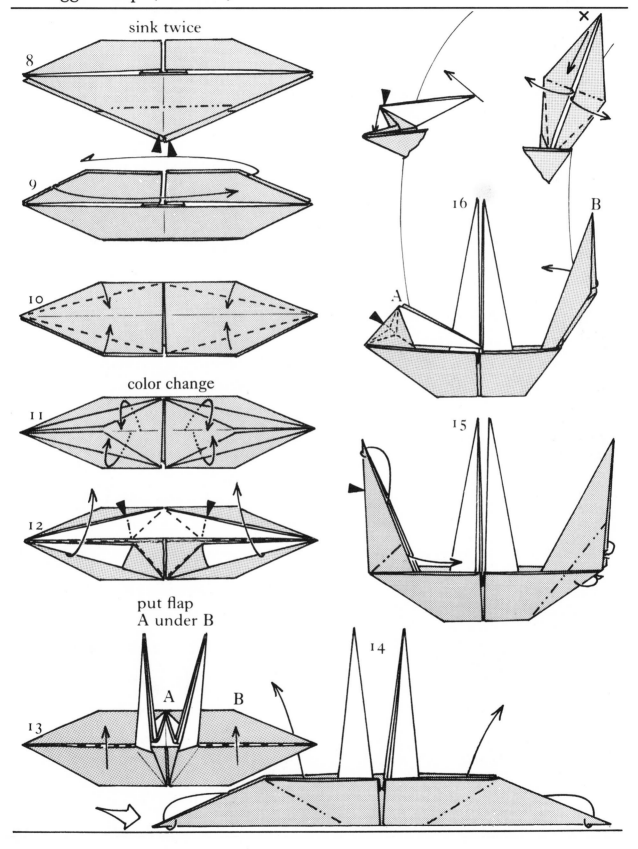

sink twice

color change

put flap
A under B

Full-rigged Ship *(continued)*

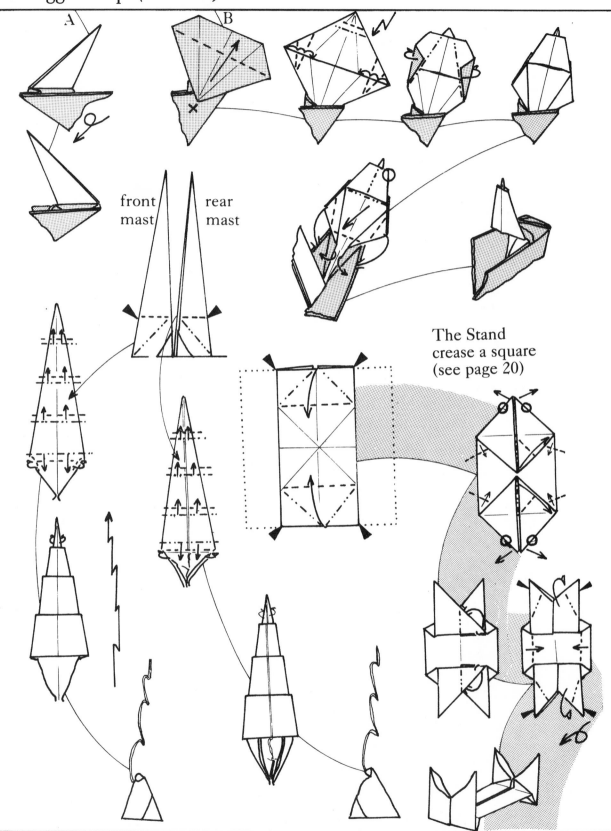

A

B

front
mast

rear
mast

The Stand
crease a square
(see page 20)

Bibliography

Here is a list of a few books on origami that are fairly easy to find:

Biddle, Steve and Megumi. *The New Origami*. London: Ebury Press, 1993.

Brill, David. *Brilliant Origami*. Briarcliff Manor, N.Y.: Japan Publications USA, 1995.

Fuse, Tomoko. *Origami Boxes*. Briarcliff Manor, N.Y.: Japan Publications USA, 1989.

Harbin, Robert. *Origami: The Art of Paperfolding*. New York: HarperCollins, 1992.

———. *Teach Yourself Origami*. Lincolnwood, Ill.: NTC Publishing Group, 1994.

Kasahara, Kunihiko. *Creative Origami*. Briarcliff Manor, N.Y.: Japan Publications USA, 1977.

———. *Origami Made Easy*. Briarcliff Manor, N.Y.: Japan Publications USA, 1973.

Kenneway, Eric. *Complete Origami*. New York: St. Martin's Press, 1987.

Montroll, John. *African Animals in Origami*. Mineola, N.Y.: Dover Publications, 1991.

———. *Origami Sculptures*. 2nd ed. Mineola, N.Y.: Dover Publications, 1991.

———. *Origami Sea Life*. Mineola, N.Y.: Dover Publications, 1991.

——— and Lillian Oppenheimer. *Origami for the Enthusiast: Step-by-Step Instructions in Over 700 Diagrams*. Mineola, N.Y.: Dover Publications, 1980.

Nakano, Dokuotei. *Origami Classroom*. Vols. 1 and 2. Briarcliff Manor, N.Y.: Japan Publications USA, 1993 and 1994.

Takahama, Toshie. *The Complete Origami Collection*. Briarcliff Manor, N.Y.: Japan Publications USA, 1996.

————. *The Joy of Origami: Ten Basic Folds Which Create Many Forms.* Briarcliff Manor, N.Y.: Japan Publications USA, 1985.

Organizations

Origami USA
15 W. 77th St.
New York, NY 10024-5912
U.S.A.

British Origami Society
2A The Chestnuts
Countesthorpe
Leicester LE8 3TL
Great Britain

Index

Anvil, 15
Archer, Ian, 22

Bases, 6
Bellows, 29
Bird Base, 6, 9, 10, 32, 47, 49, 53, 58
Birdbath, 5, 32
Birds in a Nest, 39
Blintzed Bird Base, 6
Blintz Fold, 14

Cat Stalking, 30
Christ, 6, 45
Church, 13
Color Change, 31, 59
Crawford, Patricia, 5, 18, 28, 30, 32, 35, 39, 42, 45, 47, 49, 52, 55, 58
Creases, 7
Crimps, 33, 38, 41, 48

Dart, 23
Decoration, 20
Dog, 25

Exercises, 14, 20, 23

Fancy Box, 13
Film Star, 27
Flower, 8–10
Frog Base, 55

Guillemot, 16

Harbin, Robert, 16, 26

Japanese Box, 11

Kangaroo, 52
Kenneway, Eric, 27

Lakotoi, 24
Lover's Knot, 14

Mermaid, 6, 42
Mountain Fold, 7, 34, 48

Noble, Philip, 24, 25
Nuns, 26

Octahedron, 28
Origami defined, 4

Paper, 6
Petal Fold, 6, 9, 13, 25, 30, 31, 55
Precreasing, 5, 30, 32, 35, 42, 52
Preliminary Base, 6, 8, 11, 15, 55
Procedures, 5
Push in, 6, 7, 14

Rabbit's Ears, 37, 38, 49
Reverse Folds, 6, 17, 42, 48, 51
Rohm, Fred, 6, 58

Salt Cellar, 14
Scorpion, 55
Shen, Philip, 10
Ship, 58
Sink, 6, 10, 33, 36, 37, 40, 43, 50, 53, 56, 58
Smith, John, 23
Speedboat, 22
Squash, 5, 7, 11, 12, 20, 30, 31, 55
Squirrel, 6, 35, 42
Stand, 60
Stretch, 10, 47, 49
Super-Box, 15
Swan, 47
Symbols, 5, 7

Takahama, Toshie, 21
Tetrahedron, 18

Unicorn, 49

Valley Fold, 7, 10, 23

Waterbomb Base, 6, 12, 13
Windmill Base, 13, 20

X-Ray, 7

Yacht, 21